MONSTER TRUCK

COLORING BOOK

MONSTER
TRUCK
4X4
OFF-ROAD
Ride Like the Wind

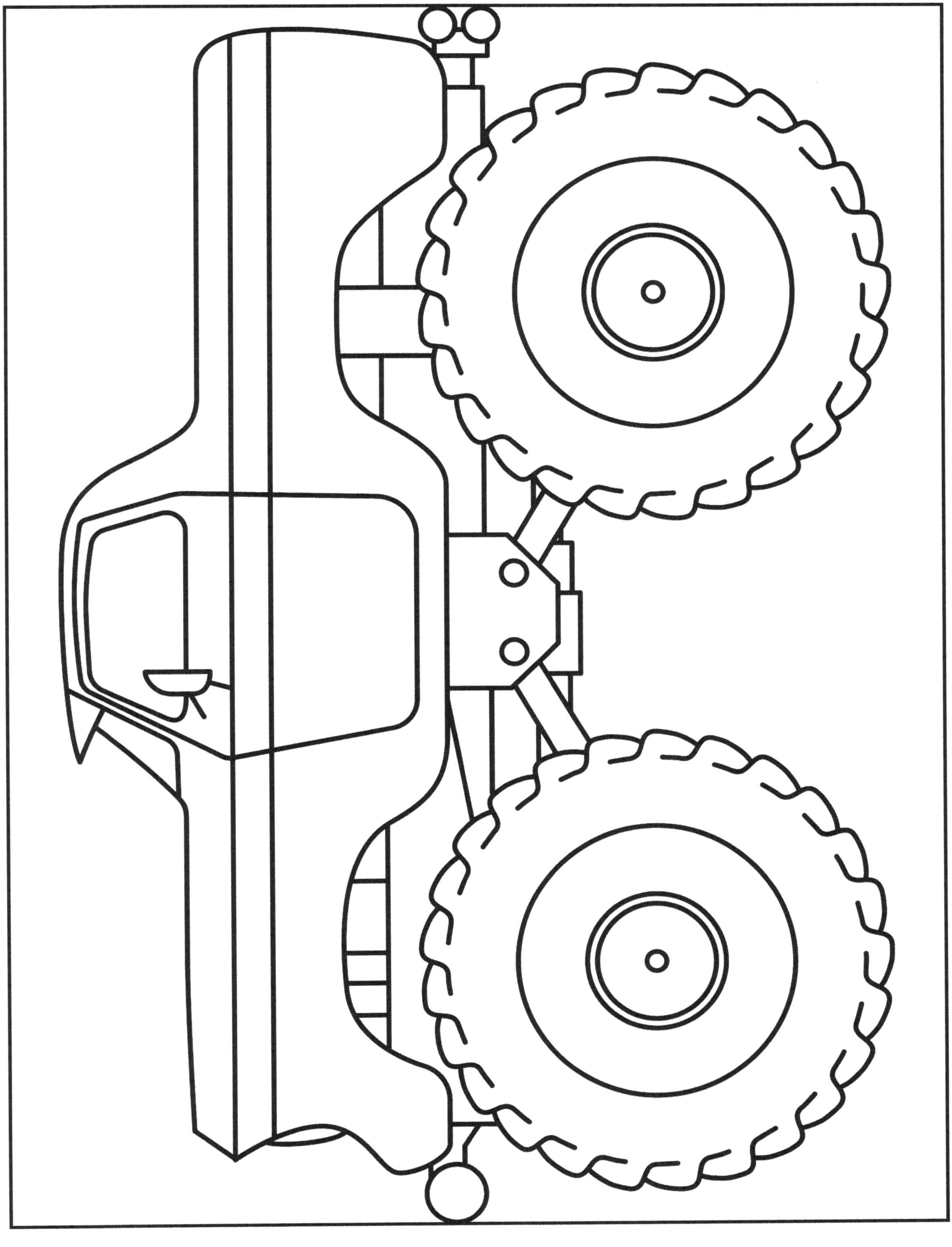

MONSTER
Truck
4 x 4

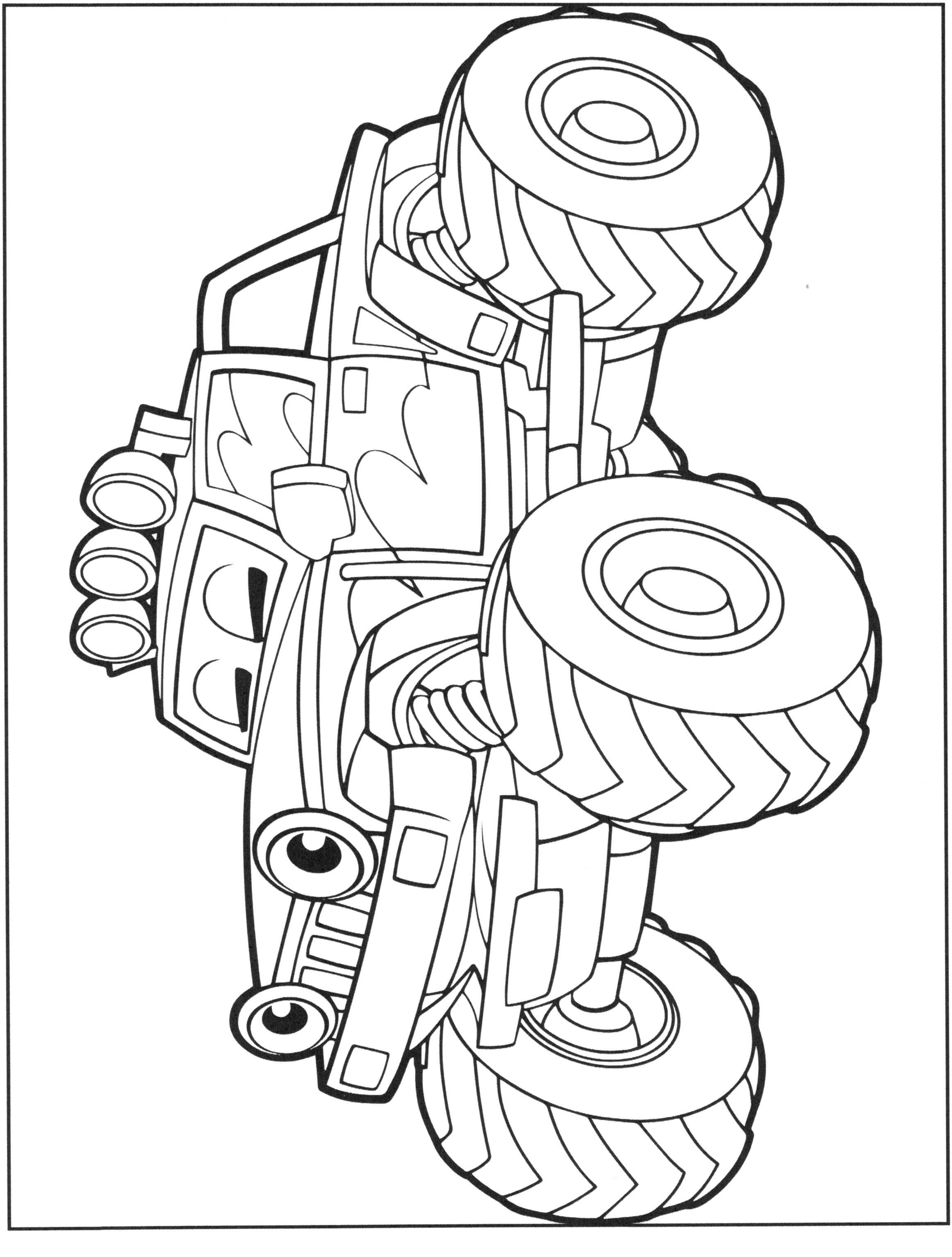

KING OF
crush

Monster
TRUCK

CRUSH

4X4

MONSTER

MONSTER
TRUCKS

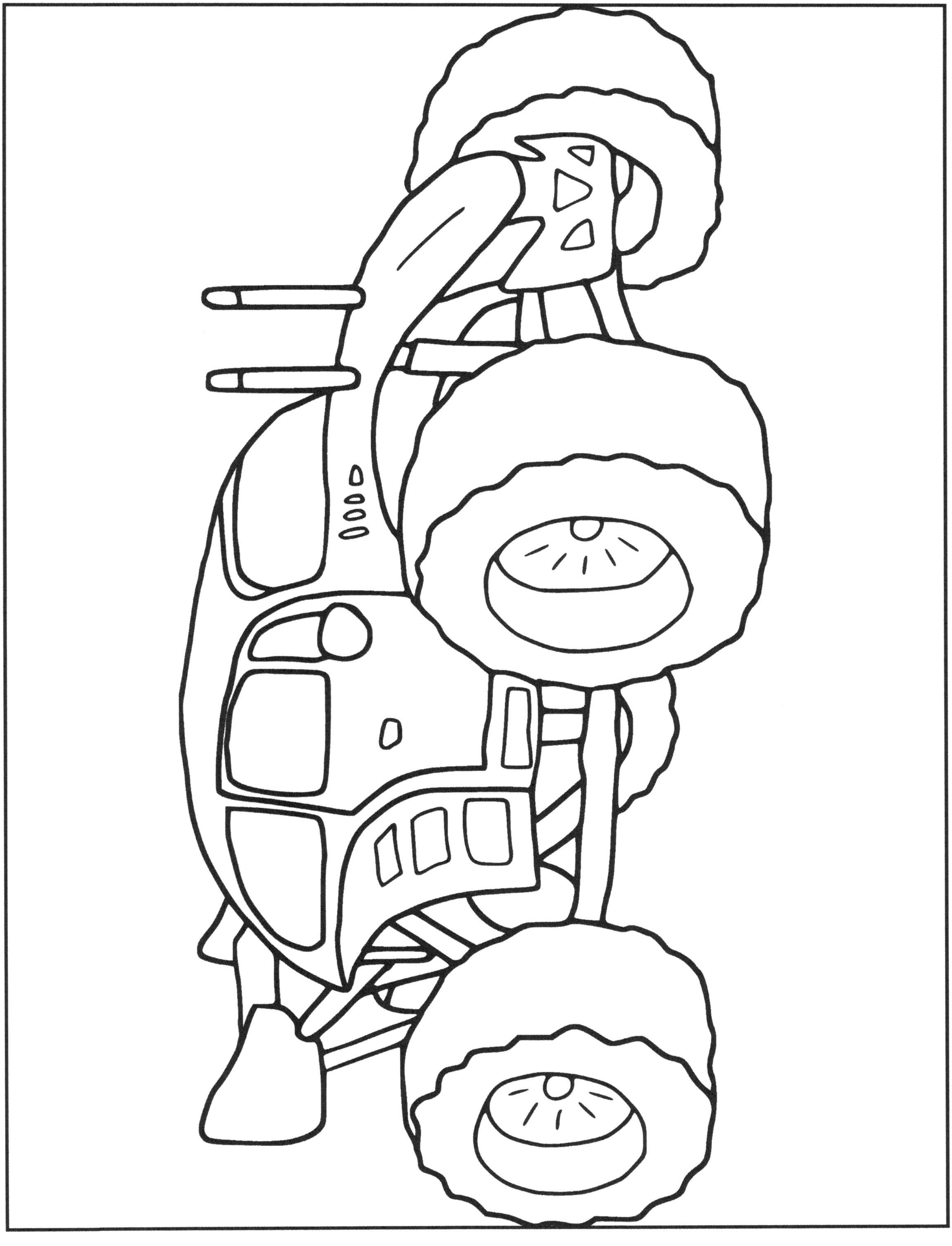

Monster TRUCK

BIG
WHEELS
4X4

Monster Truck

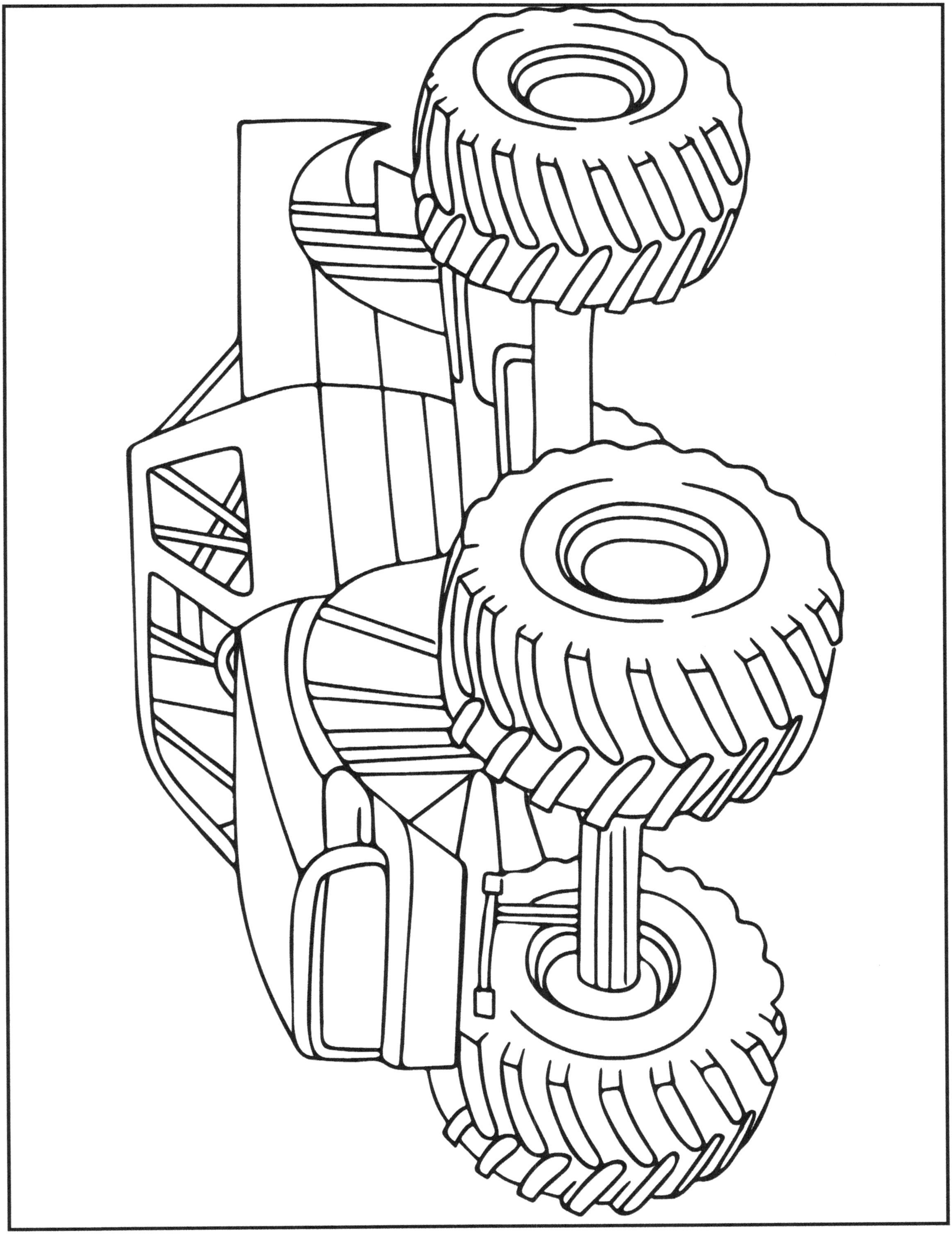

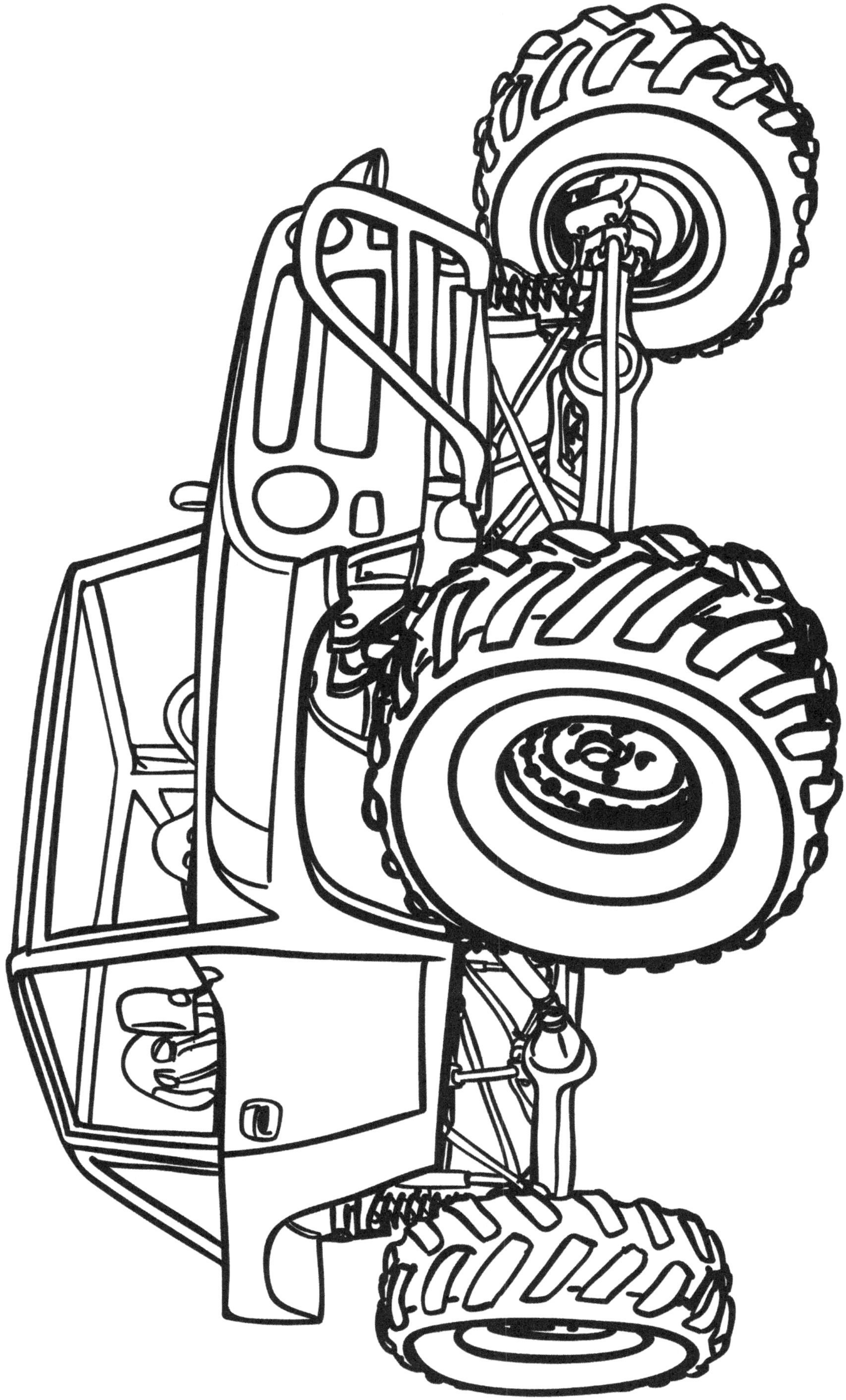

Be sure to look for more of our fur educational coloring and activity for kids!

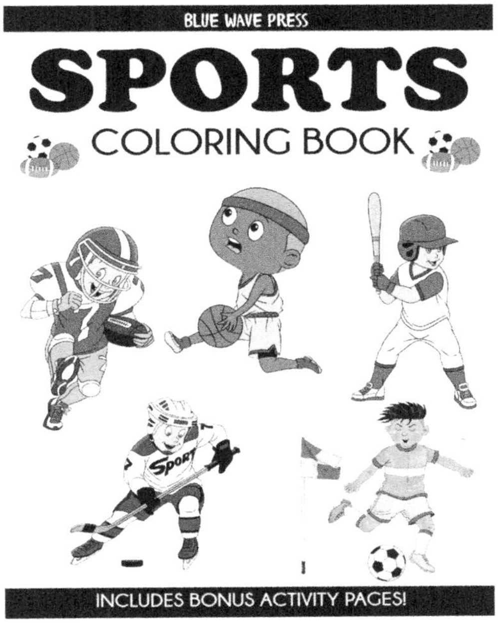

Made in the USA
Las Vegas, NV
16 December 2020

13436468R00037